W9-BNV-753

Photography by:
Arthus Bertrand, Hugo van Lawick, Günter Ziesler,
Clem Haagner, ARDEA.

HYENA FAMILY

Jane Goodall

A MADISON MINI BOOK

Published by Madison Marketing Limited.
Madison Marketing Limited holds the exclusive
license to this edition.

ISBN 1-55066-016-0

Printed in Canada

Printed on recycled paper

HYENA FAMILY

Jane Goodall
ANIMAL SERIES

Photographs selected by
Michael Neugebauer

Madison Marketing Limited

These two hyena cubs are named Sauce and Pickle. Baggage, their mother, is nearby. A few months ago they were black all over but now, at five months old, their coats are getting paler and spotted. Sauce and Pickle are full of energy and love to play. Sometimes they have a tug-of-war with a stick or a big feather.

Suddenly a large hyena approaches. I know it's a female because she's so big. Female hyenas are bigger and stronger than males. This is Bloody Mary, the "boss". There are about 50 hyenas in her clan. Bloody Mary is carrying something in her mouth. When she gets close I can see that it's one of her two cubs.

When she gets to the den she drops him beside Sauce and Pickle. Baggage hurries towards Bloody Mary and the two friends greet, hyena fashion. Each raises one back leg and, at the same time, sniffs around under the other's leg. Sauce and Pickle greet the boss in the same way. Then Bloody Mary sets off in the direction from which she came.

I follow her. Soon we arrive at her den. One small black cub is lying there, looking very much alone. She picks him up and carries him back to the others.
I know why she is moving her babies. Yesterday I saw a large lion lying almost on top of her den. She couldn't go to her cubs until he left.

All is peaceful at the new den. The two tiny cubs go sit at the entrance. Bloody Mary lies near Baggage. Suddenly we hear the strange whooping calls of other hyenas. The two mothers jump up and run towards the sounds, and I follow. Their tails are bristling and held straight up in the air. This means they're feeling aggressive.

We meet three adult hyenas and they all greet each other. There is the remains of a lion's kill nearby. Bloody Mary runs at a vulture, who is feeding. But only a few bones are left.

By now the sun has gone but there is a big moon. It's easy to follow the hyenas in the silvery light. They chase a herd of wildebeest. The hyenas pause, tails curled with excitement before rushing in to the kill. I hate to watch – but the hyenas have to eat. A little jackal appears, hoping for a share.

What a commotion once the prey is dead! They growl and whoop and make wild giggling sounds. Other hyenas of the clan hear them, and run to join in. Soon there are 33 hyenas, all leaping over one another to get closer to the meat.

The noise attracts the hyenas of a neighboring clan. Their eyes shine in the lights of my car. As more of them arrive they get bold and take over the remains of the kill, driving Bloody Mary's clan away.

By sunrise the hunters are back with their families.

While we've been gone other cubs have arrived at the den. They are about the same age as Sauce and Pickle, some a bit older. The oldest one is about 18 months. He is being weaned. When his mother arrives he tries to suckle, but she won't let him. He whines and cries like a baby, till she licks him with her rough tongue. Then he is quiet, loving it.

This morning more hyenas come visiting. Later another adult comes to visit and greets Bloody Mary as she lies near the den. One black cub plays with an older friend.

When the sun rises high and it gets hot, Sauce and Pickle go down into the den with the two black cubs. The older cubs wander back to their own dens to spend the day resting. And the adults, in little groups of friends, go off to rest too. If it's hot they will lie in pools of water, or push into the reeds around the lake. I drive away from the den. I need rest, too.

JANE GOODALL has shared her important discoveries and her love of animals with millions of people around the world through books, films and lectures. She has founded ongoing research and educational institutes on two continents, and is one of the world's most acclaimed naturalists.

The Jane Goodall Institute for Wildlife
Research, Education and Conservation
P.O. Box 41720, Tucson, AZ 85717 U.S.A.

The Jane Goodall Institute — Canada
P.O. Box 3125, Station "C"
Ottawa, Ontario K1Y 4J4 Canada

The Jane Goodall Institute — U.K.
15 Clarendon Park
Lymington, Hants S041 8AX United Kingdom